Playing Popular Piano

Neil Thomas has played in numerous pop and jazz groups, dance bands, and orchestras, and as a solo pianist. A former musical and cabaret director of the Cambridge Footlights Club at Cambridge University, he has written and arranged music and songs as well as performed them.

Playing Popular Piano

NEIL THOMAS

A SPECTRUM BOOK

Prentice-Hall, Inc., Englewood Cliffs, New Jersey 07632

Library of Congress Cataloging in Publication Data

Thomas, Neil.
    Playing popular piano.

    Method.
    "A Spectrum Book."
    1. Piano—Methods (Jazz)   2. Harmony, Keyboard.
3. Improvisation (Music)   I. Title.
MT239.T45 1982   786.3'041   82-10220
ISBN 0-13-683052-8
ISBN 0-13-683045-5 (pbk.)

This book can be made available to businesses
and organizations at a special discount when ordered
in large quantities. Contact:
Prentice-Hall, Inc.; General Book Marketing;
Special Sales Division; Englewood Cliffs, New Jersey 07632

Originally published by Pan Books Ltd. Copyright © 1980 by Neil Thomas.
Revised American Edition © 1982 by Granta Editions Ltd. and Neil Thomas.

ISBN 0-13-683052-8
ISBN 0-13-683045-5 {PBK.}

10 9 8 7 6 5 4 3 2 1

Editorial/production supervision by Alberta Boddy
Page layout by Maria Carella
Cover design by Jeannette Jacobs
Manufacturing buyer: Cathie Lenard

PRENTICE-HALL INTERNATIONAL, INC., *London*
PRENTICE-HALL OF AUSTRALIA PTY. LIMITED, *Sydney*
PRENTICE-HALL CANADA, INC., *Toronto*
PRENTICE-HALL OF INDIA PRIVATE LIMITED, *New Delhi*
PRENTICE-HALL OF JAPAN, INC., *Tokyo*
PRENTICE-HALL OF SOUTHEAST ASIA PTE. LTD., *Singapore*
WHITEHALL BOOKS LIMITED, *Wellington, New Zealand*
EDITORA PRENTICE-HALL DO BRASIL LTDA, *Rio de Janeiro*

Contents

Preface

The aims of this book are:

1. To enable an individual to understand and play chords on the piano; and to use chords:
2. to play the piano from sheet music;
3. to make playing by ear a possibility;
4. to understand the basis for improvisation;
5. to appreciate more fully the structure of music.

All pop and jazz musicians think in chords—it is therefore essential to be able to do the same in order to create the right sounds.

The book is aimed at all those who want to play popular piano and who may be drawn from the following:

1. Those who had piano lessons earlier in their lives but since have "lapsed" and who now want to return to the piano to play tunes and songs they like. Some will have forgotten more details than others and here the Basic Review Course provided will help;

2. Those beginners (possibly who play other instruments) who wish to learn to play popular piano. They may be able to play a one note melody line (violinists, clarinetists, saxophonists, etc.) or have a knowledge of chords (guitarists). The Basic Review Course and the rest of the book will enable them to play the piano by chords;

3. Those who are able to play classical music but want to play more popular pieces and not be so tied to music, so that they can use chords to play by ear or to play jazz.

This book has advantages over the other instructional books. It gives a system for working out chords, whereas other books tend to show chords diagrammatically, intending a memorization of chord principles.

For too long the piano has been taught as if it were an object that must be mastered by the pupil. This approach can, and does, lead to frustration. The piano is a piece of complex machinery, but far from your having to serve it by getting your fingers onto the right notes, it should be used as a means to express yourself musically. Chords lead to a closer relationship with the piano by making the amorphous mass of music theory and the jumble of black dots more comprehensible and the instrument itself more approachable.

Acknowledgments

We are grateful to the following publishers for their kind permission to use extracts from the works below:

AUTUMN LEAVES (Kosma/Prevert/Mercer)

© 1947 Enoch and Cie (France)
Reproduced by permission of Peter Maurice Co. Ltd.
138–140 Charing Cross Road, London WC2H 0LD

BODY AND SOUL

Music by John W. Green
Words by Robert Sour, Edward Heyman, and Frank Eyton

© 1930 Chappell Co. Ltd. & Harms Inc.
Reproduction by kind permission of Chappell Music Ltd.

GREASE
from the film GREASE
Music and Words by Barry Gibb

© 1978 Brothers Gibb B. V.
Stigwood Music Inc. Unichappell Music Inc. administers for
  World Rights
Reproduction by kind permission Chappell Music Ltd.
  (on behalf of RSO Publishing Ltd.)

How to Use This Book

ASSUMPTIONS
AND THE BASIC REVISION COURSE

The main portion of the book is written with the following assumptions; that the reader has the following:

1. a basic knowledge of the names of the notes and their positions on the piano;
2. an ability to read a one note melody line—albeit slowly;
3. some acquaintance with sharps and flats.

However, reference to the Basic Review Course in Appendix I will provide the necessary information.

LESSON FORMAT

The book is set out in lesson form, which should be followed by proceeding from lesson to lesson at a reasonably steady pace—returning to earlier portions of reading ahead as is necessary or desired.

Each lesson is self-explanatory with a summary given at the end of each. The first two lessons contain the basic theory itself. Once these are understood, the wide application of chords is straightforward—and a lot easier than by having to memorize chord shapes.

EXAMPLES

Examples of chords are given in a few different keys to show the application of the system and to reduce any fear of flats or sharps. These examples of chords, as well as the various exercises, should be played on the piano as the book is read.

MUSIC

When working from this book, the reader should buy suitable sheet or album music (if some is not already available) and apply the newfound knowledge to playing from this sheet music, by using the approaches outlined.

The sort of music needed will have chord symbols (*see* Chord symbol chart, Appendix II), but any type of music will do; it can be rock'n'roll, punk, new wave, or old standards, etc.

Introduction: Chords and What They Can Do

THE BASIS OF MUSIC

Chords are the basis of music. Understanding them is not difficult.

Harmonizing is, in effect, the adding of notes below the melody, resulting in playing or singing music in chords. This is sometimes done subconsciously or, perhaps it is fairer to say, without an understanding of the structure of the music that is being created.

Any combination of notes played together is a chord. It is to meet the difficulties of the building up of chords to surround a tune, or of the breaking down of a piece of music into its constituent chords, that these lessons have been devised.

It may be obvious, but it is still worth pointing out, that all pieces of music—jazz, pop, progressive and classical—can be broken down into chords; variations on a melody are based on the same sequence of chords.

If an individual can understand and use chords, it is easier to play from sheet music or by ear and such an understanding is essential for improvising.

TAKING A SONG APART

Pick any song or tune that you have heard being played in an effortless and flowing style by a jazz pianist. When he is

Servile Chords

playing it in its recognizable form he is thinking of it as a collection of chords in a certain sequence; when he is improvising, he is still thinking of those same chords and these then govern to a greater or lesser extent the notes played by the right hand in improvising, and by the left hand in support.

It is possible to take any classical piece of music and analyze it into the chords that underpin both the statement of theme and the endless variations that stem from it. Looked at this way even "My Country 'Tis of Thee" is just a bunch of servile chords under a well-known tune.

FAMILIARITY WITH CERTAIN FUNDAMENTAL CHORDS AND PLAYING BY EAR

The three chord trick and more
This is familiar territory to guitarists who deal with chords more obviously than pianists do. They find that learning a new song means learning words and a tune, but that the same three or four chords keep recurring. At worst it only means the same chords in a different sequence. This applies to most rock'n roll songs, 12 bar blues, jazz pieces, and many folk and popular songs.

Chord shapes
Again, guitarists know that in many instances, by keeping the same grouping of fingers in the left hand but sliding it up and down the neck of the guitar, the same chord shape can be used to play the equivalent chord in different keys. The intervals between the notes of the chords stay the same, but the key changes because you start on different notes. This can be applied to the piano.

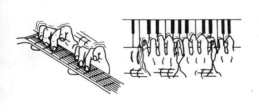

What this means to the pianists
There are certain basic chords (easily switched from key to key) that accommodate a lot of tunes. The chord shapes themselves can be understood using a straightforward system.

These easily understood and common chords offer infinite scope in supporting melodies and are the areas in any key which provide the surest and commonest harmonies around tunes.

With a knowledge of chord shapes and the ability to read a one note melody line, sheet music is much easier to play.

But more than this, it means that playing by ear or playing jazz is not such a mystery after all. Some pianists pick out a tune and subconsciously (even with some fumbling) use the same recurring chord sequences. Others play a tune and work out the harmonies by thinking, "Well, the next chord is probably . . ." any one of the commoner chords that contains the melody note. Then what governs the sequence is of course whether it sounds "right."

Playing by ear
If anybody claims to be able to play by ear, they are, whether they know it or not or whether they like it or not, really playing by chords. For this reason I believe that playing by ear can be taught and should no longer be considered as a kind of mystical gift bestowed at random on a few fortunate people.

PERSONAL EXPERIENCE

My introduction to chords
I had received piano lessons, but had not really taken to the instrument and had concentrated on the violin instead. I thus had a basic knowledge of the keyboard and could read a one note melody line.

Later while trying to learn the guitar, I realized that what I was doing with the guitar, accompanying a song with chords, could be translated onto the piano: the chords to the left hand, the voice (melody) to the right hand at the piano.

The system developed over a period of time. Besides playing by ear, I can play from sheet music with this system (using the chord symbols given) and then improvise on the chords, without being confused by the sheer mass of black dots.

Practical experience
I have at various times played in groups, bands, jazz and folk groups as well as on my own, so the system is well tested.

That it works as a teaching method has been demonstrated by various pupils. What has particularly pleased me is that, not only does the system work for others, but it also accommodates and does not stifle all different styles of playing. It gives a sure basis to a pianist's self-expression either solo or in a group.

SUMMARY

With a system of building up chords, a uniformity of chord pattern emerges. From this point, music can be broken down into, or built up from, chords and played in a more understandable way.

Sheet music becomes easier to read without fear of flats or sharps, and improvisation is easier. Because of a certain recurrence of chord sequence, it is possible to play by ear, applying a knowledge of chords to a melody.

Familiarity with chords to the point of thinking in chords and increasing dexterity in their use, which occurs over a period of time, will lead to an ability to play music you enjoy in your own style on an instrument you understand.

Lesson 1
Basic Chords

NOTE Carefully read "How to use this book." If in any doubt about any musical term used, refer to Appendix I (Basic review course) or Appendix II (Chord symbol chart).

Basic chords should be thought of as comprising *three notes* and taking their name from the bottom note (the root). The intervals between these three notes are varied to give the different basic chords required.

I think of there being four basic chords: major, minor, diminished, and augmented. These are dealt with in this lesson. The next lesson deals with notes added to chords to make up remaining chords.

In following this lesson, if you have any doubts or difficulties with scales or keys, please refer to the Basic review course, Appendix I. I use chord symbols based on the key of C as examples of symbols used to denote chords, but the name of any note could be substituted before the symbol, to describe the same chord on that note. This is made clear in the symbol chart in Appendix II. All basic chords in all keys are built up in the same way and the examples given illustrate the application of this system.

MAJOR CHORDS (SYMBOL: C)

To obtain the three notes of the chord of C major, first play the major scale of C as follows:

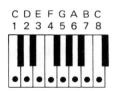

Major Chord

Counting from the bottom take the first, C; the third, E; the fifth, G; and play the chord of C major:

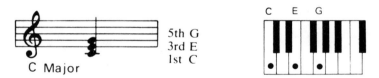

C Major

5th G
3rd E
1st C

Put another way, the intervals are a major third and a major fifth between these notes which are taken from the major scale of C:

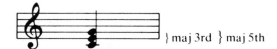

} maj 3rd } maj 5th

In half steps the inclusive gaps between the notes are:

} 4 **half steps**
} 5 **half steps** } 8

NOTE This may help in counting to the notes, but the easiest way is to think of the major scale and take the third and fifth notes.

In fingering, to help you to think of the first, third, and fifth notes, use the right hand and play the notes as follows:

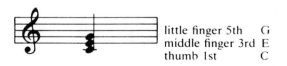

little finger 5th   G
middle finger 3rd   E
thumb 1st   C

This basic principle applies to any major chord: think first of the scale, then take the first, third, and fifth notes of that scale to get the major chord.

With the left hand, the fingering (using the chord of C major as an example) is as follows:

Use this, or any other convenient fingering, in playing chords with right or the left hand from any of the examples given. It is important that the chord examples given are tried out using each hand, particularly the left hand, which will often be used to play the supporting chords to the melody on improvisation played with the right hand.

EXAMPLES

Chord of F major

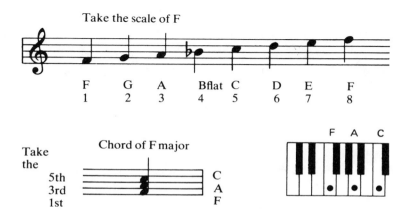

Chord of G major

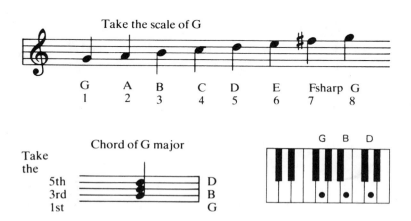

Now try the chords of D major, A major, E♭ major by first playing the major scales of D, A, and E♭ and taking the first, third, and fifth notes from each to get the major chords. You should end up with these chords:

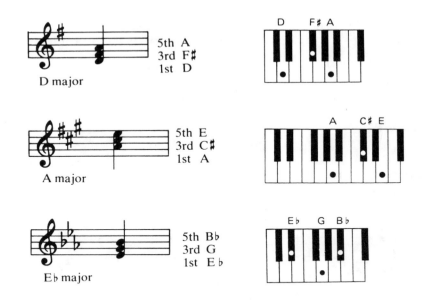

TO RECAP A major chord comprises the first, third, and fifth notes of the major scale that takes its name from the bottom note (the root). To play a major chord, therefore, it is best to first play the major scale and then take the appropriate notes. This is only necessary at the early stages. If you have any difficulty with any scales the information in the Basic review course (Appendix I) will help. Once you can work out a major chord, all the rest will follow.

MINOR CHORDS
(SYMBOLS: Cm, C min)

To get a *minor chord* take any major chord and *lower the middle note*. This is called *lowering the third*. Thus to play C minor:

The interval between the first and third is altered from a major third to a minor third. As with C minor, all other minor chords can be similarly obtained from the corresponding major.

Minor Chord

EXAMPLES

F minor

First play F major   *Lower the third*   F minor

5th C
3rd A
1st F

C
Ab
F

F Ab C

G minor

First play G major   *Lower the third*   G minor

5th D
3rd B
1st G

D
Bb
G

G Bb D

Eb minor

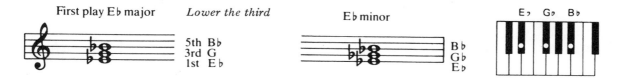

First play Eb major   *Lower the third*   Eb minor

5th Bb
3rd G
1st Eb

Bb
Gb
Eb

Eb Gb Bb

and so on with every major chord, *lower the third* to get the *minor chord* from the root note.

DIMINISHED CHORDS
(SYMBOLS: C°, C⁻, C dim)

To get a *diminished chord*, take any major chord and *lower (diminish) the third and the fifth notes.*

Diminished Chord

C diminished

Similarly, to obtain any other diminished chord, take the major and *lower the third and fifth.*

D diminished

A diminished

B♭ diminished

NOTE Diminished chords usually add the sixth note. So for the full sound the chord of C diminished would be:

AUGMENTED CHORDS
(SYMBOLS: C⁺, C⁺⁵, C aug)

Augmented Chord

To get an *augmented chord,* take any major chord and *raise (augment) the fifth* to get the augmented chord. Thus to play C augmented:

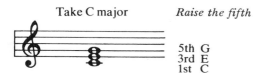
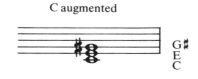
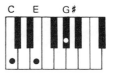

Similarly to obtain any other augmented chord, take the major chord and *raise the fifth:*

F augmented

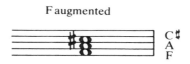
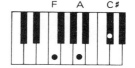

G augmented

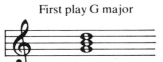

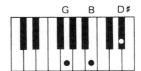

E♭ augmented

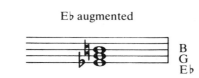
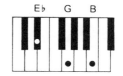

15

SUMMARY

1. Think of there being four basic chords.
2. Each chord has three notes.
3. Each chord takes its name from the root.
4. We obtain the basic chords in all the different keys as follows:

a. *major chords:* play the first, third, and fifth notes of the major scale that runs from the root; e.g. C major:

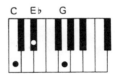

b. *minor chords:* take the major chord then *lower the third;* e.g. C minor:

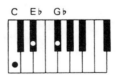

c. *diminished chords:* take the major chord then *lower the third and fifth;* e.g. C diminished:

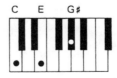

d. *augmented chords:* take the major chord then *raise the fifth;* e.g. C augmented:

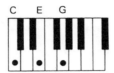

EXERCISES

Try playing, however slowly, the following pieces, using the right hand to play the melody line and the left hand to play the chords—play the chord wherever the symbol is written.

When the Saints

On Top of Old Smoky

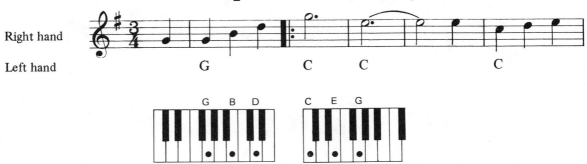

Lesson 2

The Remaining Chords

All remaining chords are variations made to the basic chords and should be thought of as being made up of basic chords, with other notes being added to them.

THE SIXTH CHORD
(SYMBOLS: C 6, C sixth)

The note added in playing a sixth chord is the *sixth note* of the major scale that runs from, and takes its name from the root note of, the basic chord.

C sixth

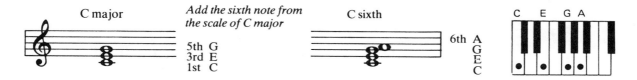

The note A that is added is the sixth note of the scale of C.

F sixth

Applying this to other major chords, F sixth is the chord of F major with the sixth note from the scale of F being added:

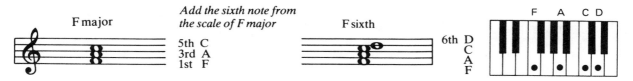

G sixth

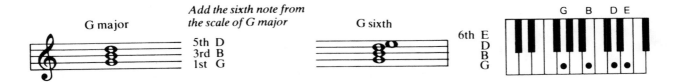

The sixth chord gives a very sweet sound, which is used very often in older popular songs, sometimes as the final chord.

Just as sixth notes can be added to major chords, so they can be added to minor and diminished chords, but rarely to augmented chords unless a discordant sound is required.

Minor chords with added sixths
(Symbols: C min 6 or Cm6)

Again, as for all sixth chords, it should be remembered that the sixth note to be added is the sixth note from the scale of C major. Thus the chord of C minor sixth is:

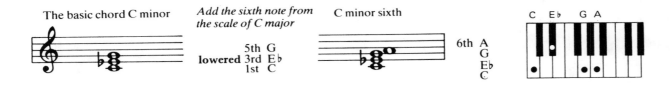

The sixth note added is A from the major scale of C, as has been seen. It should also be noted that in the symbol for this chord (C min 6 or Cm6), the minor (m, or min) refers to the basic chord and not the sixth.

F minor sixth

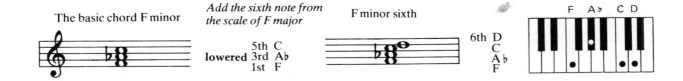

E♭ minor sixth

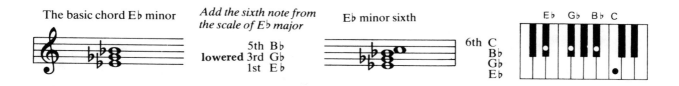

Diminished chords with sixths
(Symbols: C°, C⁻, C dim, C dim 7)

A word first about the symbols used for diminished chords. These are the same as for the basic chord of C diminished—this is because the sixth can be added to the diminished chord as required, and frequently is. The symbol C dim 7 is perhaps slightly more puzzling, but describes the diminished basic chord with an added diminished seventh—think of it as diminished from B to A in this example of C dim 7.

To play C diminished with an added sixth:

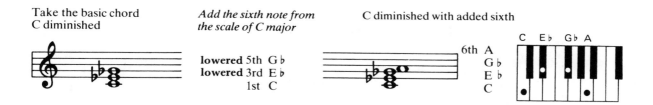

The sixth note added is the sixth note from the major scale that runs from the root note—here A is the sixth note added from the scale of C major.

Similarly, to obtain the chord of F diminished with an added sixth:

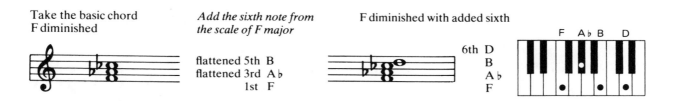

G diminished
with an added sixth

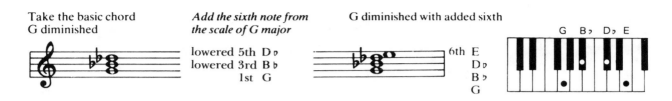

Take the basic chord G diminished	Add the sixth note from the scale of G major	G diminished with added sixth	
	lowered 5th Db		6th E
	lowered 3rd Bb		Db
	1st G		Bb
			G

THE MAJOR SEVENTH
CHORD
(SYMBOL: C maj 7)

In the symbol for the major seventh chord, the "maj" refers to the note that is added. In effect it must do, because the symbol C, *on its own,* would stand for the chord of C major. The symbol is as it is to differentiate the *major seventh chord* from the *seventh chord* explained later in this lesson.

For major seventh chords, the note added to the basic chord is the seventh note from the major scale that runs from the root of the chord.

The chord of C major seventh

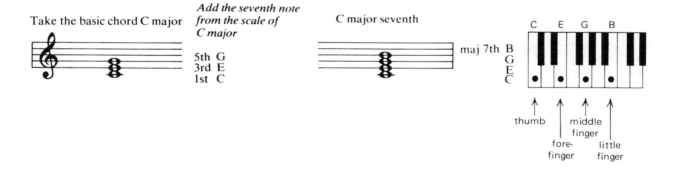

Take the basic chord C major	Add the seventh note from the scale of C major	C major seventh	
	5th G		maj 7th B
	3rd E		G
	1st C		E
			C

thumb   middle finger
fore-finger   little finger

The chord of F major seventh

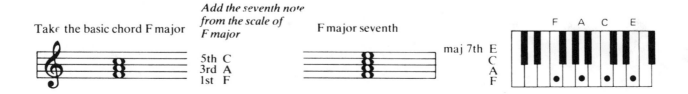

Take the basic chord F major	Add the seventh note from the scale of F major	F major seventh	
	5th C		maj 7th E
	3rd A		C
	1st F		A
			F

The major seventh note can of course be added to the other basic chords, but only if more unusual harmonies are required and the symbols would be:

> For C minor with added major seventh: C min (maj 7)
>
> For C diminished with added major seventh: C dim (maj 7) or C$^-$ (maj 7) or C° (maj 7)
>
> For C augmented with added major seventh: C aug (maj 7) or C^{+5} (maj 7) or C♯^{5} (maj 7)

But for each, the note added is the seventh note of the major scale running from the root.

THE SEVENTH CHORD
(SYMBOLS: C7, C seventh)

The distinction between major seventh and seventh chords can be slightly confusing at first, apparently confounding the simple approach of adding notes to chords. It does not in fact break any basic rules, so long as it is clearly remembered that *C seventh* is the shorthand way of writing the chord of C major plus the *lowered seventh* note of the scale of C major.

This is made more logical by remembering that there is a chord called *C major seventh* which is made up of the basic chord of C major plus the note which is the major seventh note of the scale of C major.

Think then that the seventh means *lowered seventh,* as opposed to the major seventh, of the scale that runs from the root of the chord to be played.

The chord of C seventh

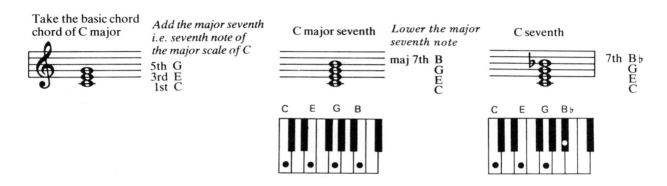

By playing these chords, you will be able to hear the difference between the major seventh and the seventh. The latter has a distinctly off-key sound which is more "dominating" than the major seventh. The seventh chord is referred to in music theory as the dominant seventh, but for other reasons.

Applying the principle then to chords in other keys, the major seventh and seventh chords are formed as follows:

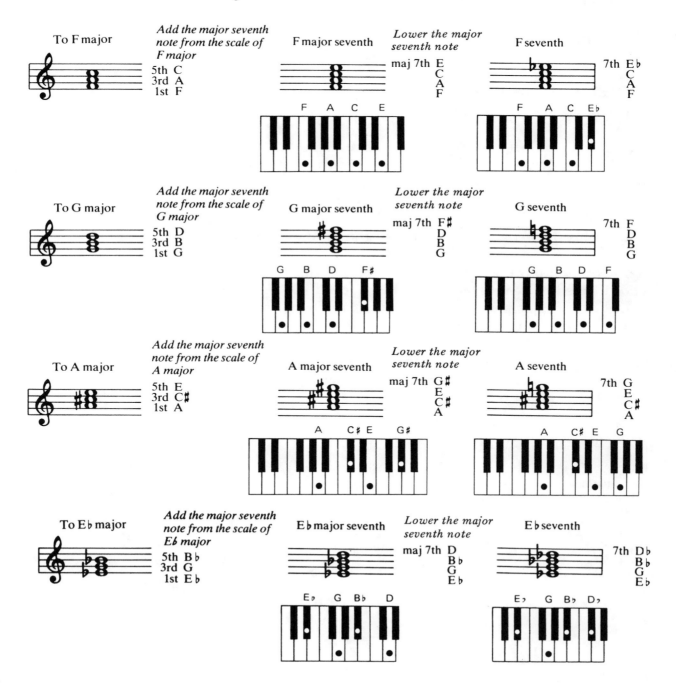

It is the symbol denoting a *major seventh* that adds the major seventh note from the scale that runs from the root, while the symbol denoting a *seventh* refers to the lowered seventh note of the major scale being added to the basic chord.

Minor chords with added sevenths (Symbols: Cm7, C min 7)

We have seen that in writing the symbol C major seventh, the major describes how the seventh is to be played. The symbol C seventh, then, denotes the chord of C major with a lowered seventh note. If we write C minor seventh, the word *minor* describes the basic chord because the symbol seventh *of itself* means a lowered seventh note.

Thus the chord C minor seventh is the chord of C minor plus the lowered seventh note of the major scale of C:

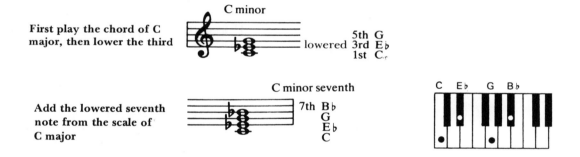

First play the chord of C major, then lower the third — C minor — lowered 5th G / 3rd E♭ / 1st C

Add the lowered seventh note from the scale of C major — C minor seventh — 7th B♭ / G / E♭ / C

The chord of F minor seventh

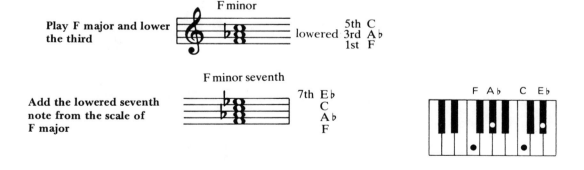

Play F major and lower the third — F minor — lowered 5th C / 3rd A♭ / 1st F

Add the lowered seventh note from the scale of F major — F minor seventh — 7th E♭ / C / A♭ / F

The chord of G minor seventh

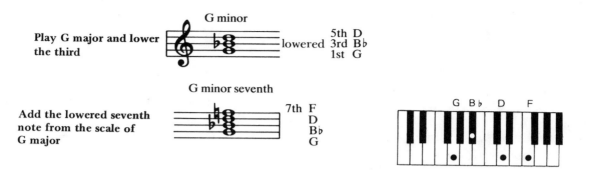

Play G major and lower the third

G minor

lowered 5th D 3rd B♭ 1st G

Add the lowered seventh note from the scale of G major

G minor seventh

7th F
D
B♭
G

Sevenths (that means *lowered sevenths!*) can be added to the other basic chords:

To augmented chords (symbols: C⁷+⁵, C⁷♯⁵, C aug 7), take the basic augmented chord and add the flattened seventh note of the scale that runs from the root.

To diminished chords (symbols: C⁻⁽⁷⁾, C°⁽⁷⁾, C dim ⁽⁷⁾), take the basic diminished chord and add the lowered seventh note of the scale that runs from the root.

TO RECAP Unless a major seventh is written as such, the seventh means the lowered seventh note of the major scale.

Thus:

C major seventh (symbol: C maj7) is C major plus the major seventh note from the scale of C major

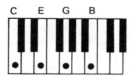

C seventh (symbol: C7) is C major plus the lowered seventh note from the scale of C major

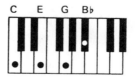

C minor seventh (symbol: Cm7 or Cmin7) is C minor plus the lowered seventh note from the scale of C major

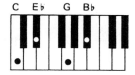

and so on.

THE NINTH CHORD
(SYMBOLS: C9, C ninth)

To obtain a ninth chord, take the basic chord, major, minor, diminished, or augmented and add the ninth note of the major scale that runs from the root. Thus ninths with C basic chords are as follows, the ninth note added (D) being the ninth note of a two octave scale of C major:

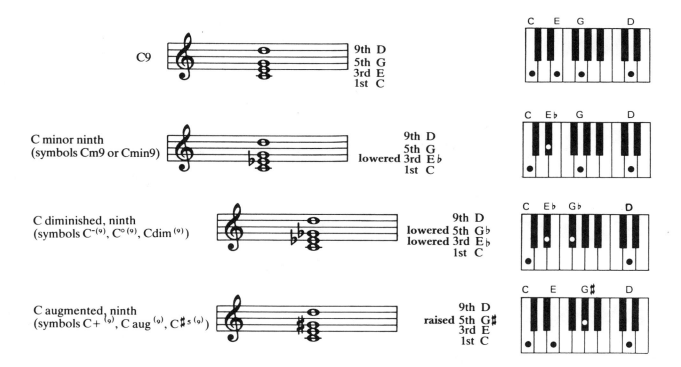

Similarly, ninths with F chords are the basic chords plus the ninth note (G) of the scale of F major:

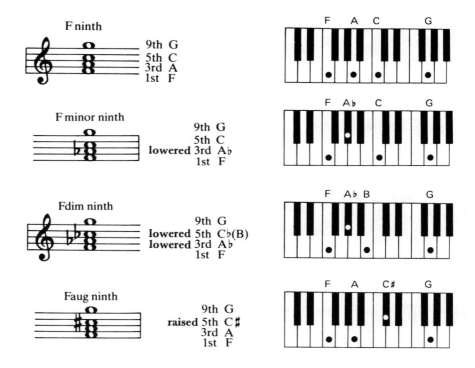

F ninth	9th G 5th C 3rd A 1st F
F minor ninth	9th G 5th C lowered 3rd A♭ 1st F
F dim ninth	9th G lowered 5th C♭(B) lowered 3rd A♭ 1st F
F aug ninth	9th G raised 5th C♯ 3rd A 1st F

and so on with ninth chords based on all other basic chords.

Usually, the ninth is a combination chord taking in the seventh (i.e. the lowered seventh note) as well. In fact, the seventh can be added to ninth chords as required, even if not denoted by the chord symbol given. Sometimes the seventh is a specified addition as in the symbols:

C^9_7 where the ninth and seventh (lowered seventh!) are added to the chord of C major:

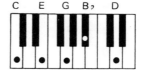

C min $^9_7$ where the ninth and seventh (lowered seventh!) are added to the chord of C minor:

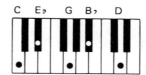

and so on for other chords.

REMAINING CHORDS

Virtually any notes can be added to the basic chords and this can be denoted by an appropriate shorthand chord symbol. This can be seen from the Symbol chart and from sheet or album music. The symbols used are self-descriptive, indicating the basic chord to be used and indicating the further note or amended further note to be added.

Thus the symbol C7 (sus 4) means the chord of C seventh plus the fourth note added (F) from the scale of C major:

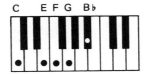

F♭⁵ means the chord of F major with the fifth note lowered

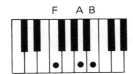

G maj 7 ⁽♭⁵⁾ means the chord of G major seventh with the fifth note lowered

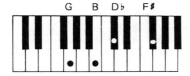

You will meet all kinds of variations of symbols in sheet music, but if you now refer to the Symbol chart in Appendix II, the full scope can be seen. You should work through the chords in the chart, playing the chords described, in C and other keys. Doing this will reinforce the basic principles, clarify the position with regard to added or altered notes, illustrate the variations in the shorthand symbols used and give familiarity in reading them.

SUMMARY

Always keep the basic chords firmly in mind:

The major chord: first, third, and fifth notes of the major scale that starts on the root, e.g. C major:

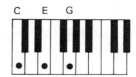

The minor chord: take the major chord and lower the third, e.g. C minor:

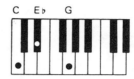

The diminished chord: take the major chord and lower the third and the fifth, e.g. C diminished:

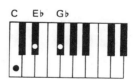

The augmented chord: take the major chord and raise the fifth, e.g. C augmented:

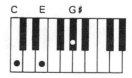

Then for other chords:

Sixths: to any of the basic chords add the sixth note of the major scale that starts on the root of the basic chord, e.g. C sixth:

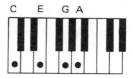

Major sevenths: add the major seventh note from the major scale that runs from the root of the basic chord to which it is to be added, e.g. C major seventh:

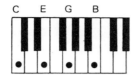

Sevenths: add the lowered seventh note from the major scale that runs from the root of the basic chord to which it is to be added, e.g. C seventh:

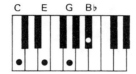

Remaining chords: add the specified notes from the major scale, or amend the specified notes to the basic or further chords, e.g. C seventh with suspended fourth:

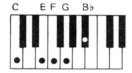

This applies to whatever range of chords—the principle runs through all keys. It is therefore possible to work out all the chords in all keys on the piano without memorizing positions. Knowing how to arrive at the notes of the chords means that they can be played with the right or left hands in the treble or bass clefs.

NOTE As these two lessons have been proceeding, you may have been applying the system to music and playing from it—the approaches outlined in Lesson 5 will help in doing this, and no harm will be done in turning ahead to that lesson.

I have put Lesson 3 and 4 at this stage because they round off the basic system and give further opportunities to practice chords before their widespread application to reading from music, playing by ear and improvising, which are the topics dealt with in Lessons 5 and 6.

Lesson 3

Inversions;
The Three Chord Trick;
Transposing

The contents of this lesson flow naturally from the previous two and lead to the next one on 12 bar blues, which has been used to bring the various strands together.

INVERSIONS

All chords can be played with the notes that make them up arranged in a different order, i.e. "inverted". So the chord of C major using the notes C, E, and G (the first, third, and fifth notes of the scale of C major) could be played as:

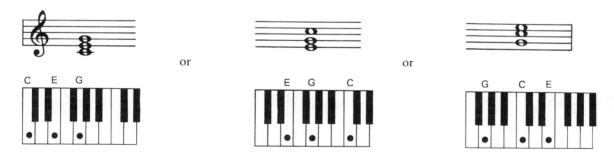

or

or

Similarly, the chord of F minor (think F major and lower the third!) could be played as:

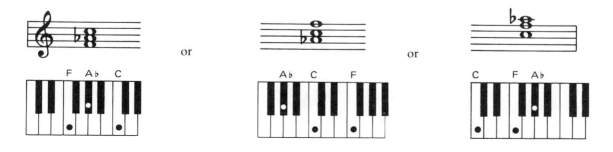

or

or

And the chord of G seventh (think G major with an added lowered seventh from the scale of G major!) could be played as:

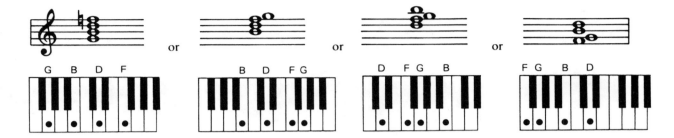

It is very useful to be able to invert chords in this way, because it makes changing from chord to chord, in either left or right hand, much easier. When familiarity with the basic chords has reached the level of being able to remember what notes make up the chords, then you will be able to arrange them in the easiest order for playing the chords specified in a piece of music.

To jump ahead a little, but to show further that thinking in chords and inversions is useful, it is often effective when playing a piece of music to:

1. play single notes (the roots of the required chords) with the left hand; these can be played as octave notes in unison as shown in the example below;

2. make up the rest of the chord by playing, with the right hand, the melody note and below that melody note, the other notes of the chord.

So the chord of C seventh under a melody note of C could be played:

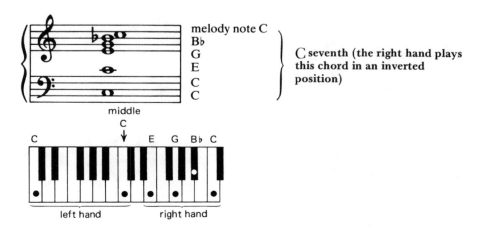

EXAMPLES

You should now practice playing chords in their different inverted forms.

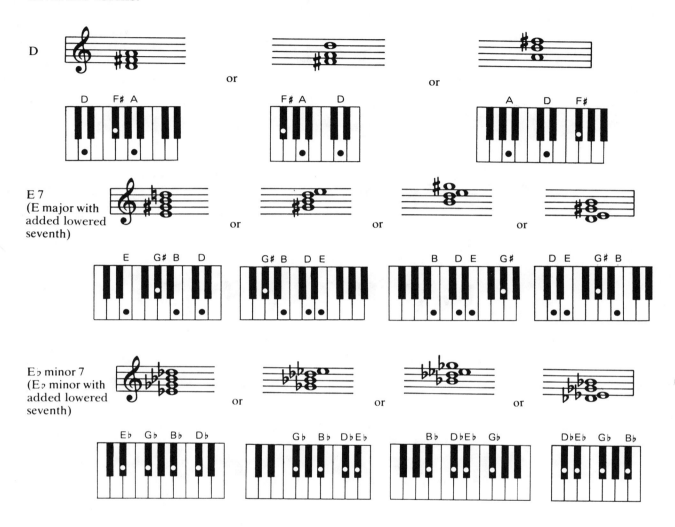

and so on for all other chords.

THE THREE CHORD TRICK

This was touched on briefly in the Introduction, but now it can be explained fully. In any key, there are only three major chords that can be built up by using only the notes of that scale to give the constituent firsts, thirds, and fifths.

This can be more readily understood by example.

Taking the key of C, the major scale is:

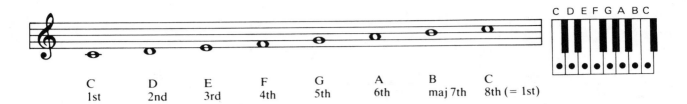

C	D	E	F	G	A	B	C
1st	2nd	3rd	4th	5th	6th	maj 7th	8th (= 1st)

Using *only the above notes* as the firsts, thirds, and fifths of chords, we get the following chords:

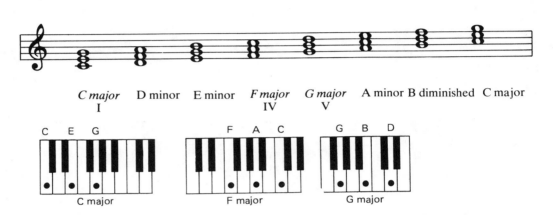

C major D minor E minor *F major* *G major* A minor B diminished C major
   I   IV   V

The only major chords produced are C, F, and G, using strictly the notes that appear in the scale of C. Thus chords based on the I, IV, and V notes of the scale give the major chords of a key.

So in the key of F, the major scale of which is:

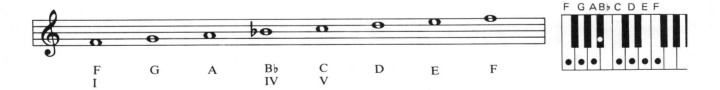

F	G	A	Bb	C	D	E	F
I			IV	V			

The major chords using only the notes of the scale of F as the firsts, thirds, and fifths of chords (the rest being minors or diminished) are:

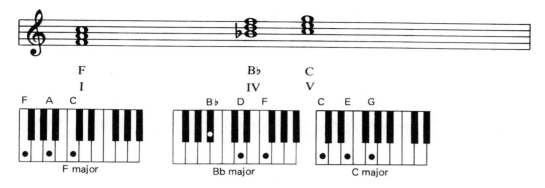

It is these three chords in any key (the I, IV, and V) that are the most common in all music, providing the surest harmonies to melodies. They are the three chords used as the basis for most 12 bar blues.

It can be seen, just as different keys merely alter the pitch of music not the basic harmonies, so F, B♭, and C as the I, IV, and V chords of the scale (key) of F correspond to C, F, and G as the I, IV, and V chords of the scale (key) of C.

TRANSPOSING

The three chord trick can be used in any key by taking the appropriate I, IV, and V chords.

This is in effect transposing chords from one key to another. The following table is an example of how to transpose the I, IV, and V chords from one key to the corresponding chords of other keys. They are all major chords.

	keys	I	IV	V	
Examples from keys with sharps	C	C	F	G	
	G	G	C	D	
	D	D	G	A	
	A	A	D	E	The three-chord trick in different keys
Examples from keys with flats	F	F	B♭	C	
	B♭	B♭	E♭	F	
	E♭	E♭	A♭	B♭	

So, to get the corresponding chords of A, D, and E (in the key of A) in the key of Eb, take the I, IV, and V chords of Eb, Ab, and Bb.

Reference should now be made to the Transposing chart in Appendix III to see how to transpose any note or chord that appears in a piece of music written in a certain key, to the relevant note or chord required if the piece is to be played in a different key.

SUMMARY

Familiarity with the fundamental positions of basic and other chords enables inversions to be played. This makes changing from chord to chord easier and gives flexibility in harmonization. For example, the following inversions of the specified chords show how inversions can be used to help the chord progression lie under the hand and cut down the need to move around the keyboard:

Cm7   F7   Cm7

Inversions are often used in jazz and, for example, the Block chord piano style of George Shearing is typified by the left hand playing, at its simplest, the octave of the melody note with the notes added in between forming a progression of chords being played in their inversions. Thus:

C6 Cmaj7 C6

There are, in any key, three primary major chords based on the I, IV, and V notes of the scale. In all keys these three chords correspond to the same chords in other keys, and transposition between these chords in different keys is easy to understand. Further than this, it is fairly straightforward to transpose chords and notes to change the key of a piece of music; the Transposing chart in Appendix III will help in this.

Lesson 4
12 Bar Blues

INTRODUCTION

Various strands can be brought together and practiced in 12 bar blues. We can use this well-known structure to illustrate:

1. putting a series of chords together
2. playing inversions of chords
3. adding notes to chords to give different sounds
4. transposing
5. developing rhythm and natural feel
6. the interplay between left and right hands
7. variations around a chord sequence.

12 bar blues can be played fast or slow and, because of the "feel" that it has, lends itself to jazz, blues, rock'n roll, and pop songs. A lot of early songs were written in 12 bar blues form; boogie woogie is usually in 12 bar form. Endless fun can be had by extemporizing around the basic chords used.

WHAT IS A 12 BAR BLUES?

Basically, 12 bar blues is three chords in one key played in a set order for 12 bars.

The chords used

The three chords used are those based on the I, IV, and V notes of the scale of the key in question.

Thus

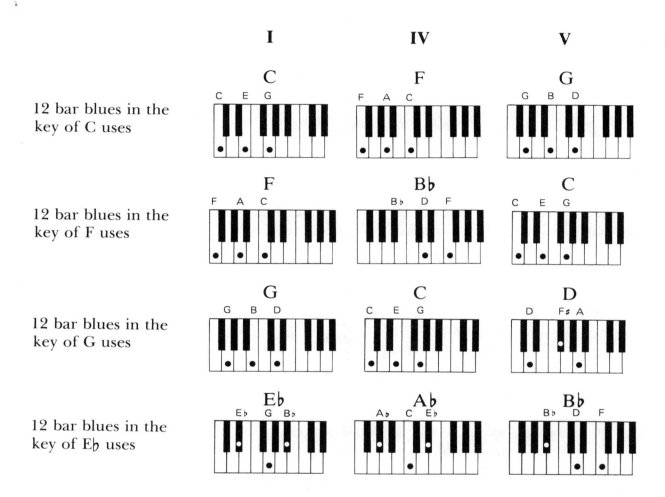

It is thus relatively easy to pick the relevant three chords out of any key for 12 bar blues in that key.

Knowing then the primary chords to be used, it can be seen that 12 bar blues could be played on other basic chords based on the same notes, or adding or amending notes to the basic chords used.

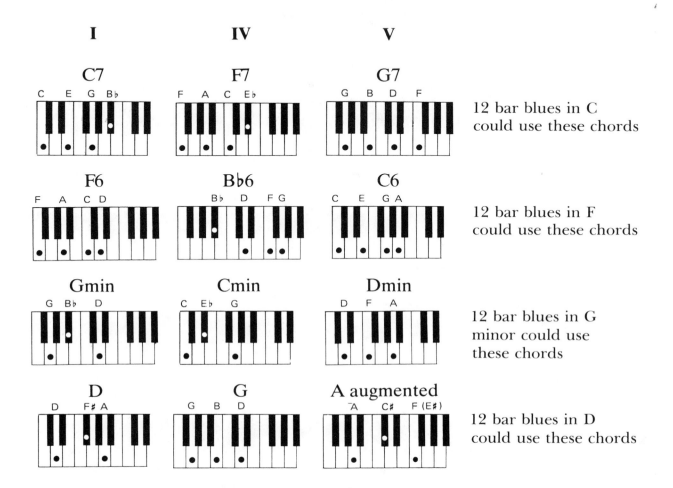

12 bar blues in C
could use these chords

12 bar blues in F
could use these chords

12 bar blues in G
minor could use
these chords

12 bar blues in D
could use these chords

and so on.

The order in which the three chords are played

Although at first sight the sequence seems rigid, it has a natural feel about it that sounds right and as a form it is much freer than it first appears. It gives infinite opportunities for improvisation.

12 bar blues means 12 bars (and using the key of C as our example) based on the three chords (I, IV, and V), played in the order shown below. Remember the same would apply to 12 bars in F, or G, or any other key.

NOTE The diagonal lines show that the same chord is to be played a further three times in each bar, to make four beats in all.

12 Bar Blues in C

4 bars on the chord of C	$\frac{4}{4}$ | C/// | C/// | C/// | C/// |
2 bars on the chord of F	| F/// | F/// |
2 bars on the chord of C	| C/// | C/// |
1 bar on the chord of G	| G/// | } (this can be two bars on
1 bar on the chord of F	| F/// | } the chord of G)
1 bar on the chord of C	| C/// |
1 bar on the chord of G	| G/// | (this could be a further bar of C)
12 bars TOTAL	

Musically, this can be written out as shown below. You should play each chord for each beat in each bar and count accordingly. This will sound rather boring at first, but if you play it over and over, getting a little faster, you will soon be able to 'feel' when the change in chord should occur. Having thus got used to the sound of 12 bar blues, and no longer having to count so rigidly, it will become apparent that by varying tempos and playing notes from the chords and additional notes in runs or other frills, you can use 12 bar blues to create your own music.

You should practice the following by using the *left hand* to play octave notes held for four beats and the *right hand* to play the chords for each of the four beats in each bar:

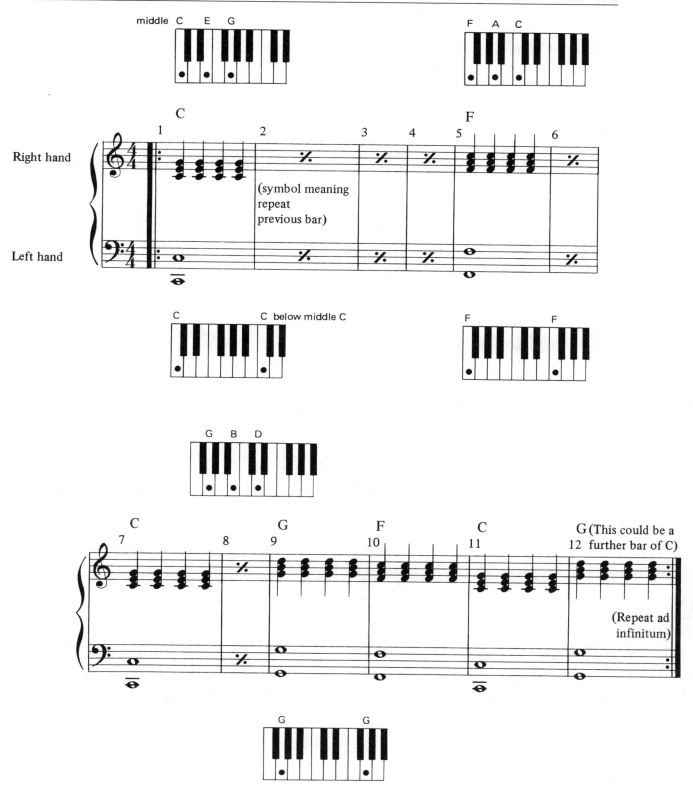

EXERCISES

Using sixth chords

For slight variation, use the chords of C6, F6, and G6 and play as follows—in the left hand play the root note held for four beats and in the right hand, an inversion of the chords played for each of the four beats in the bar:

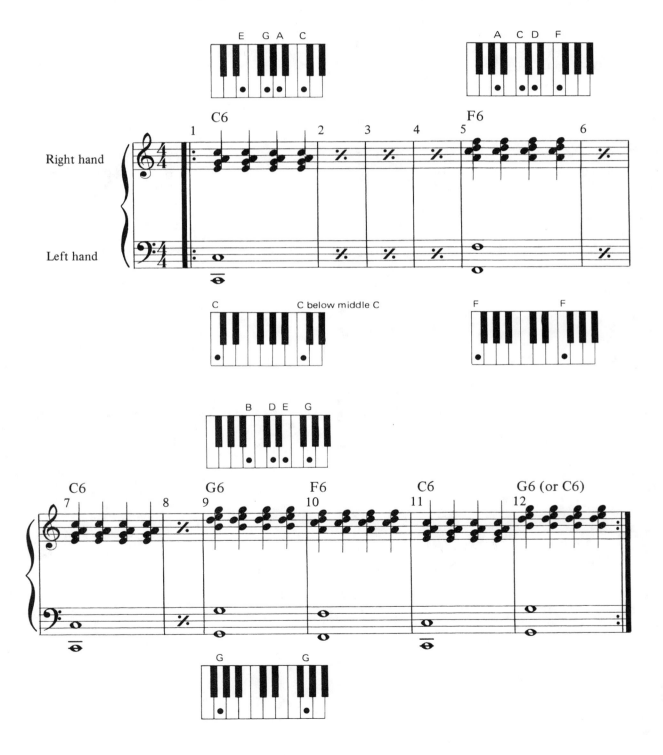

Seventh heaven?

By far the most common chord in 12 bar blues is the seventh—remember that the seventh is the basic chord plus the *lowered seventh* note of the scale running from the root.

Try playing 12 bar blues using the chords of C7, F7, and G7, substituting the seventh chords in their inverted positions for the inverted sixths in the previous exercise.

Use the sevenths in one of their inverted positions for the right hand, and again play the root with the left hand:

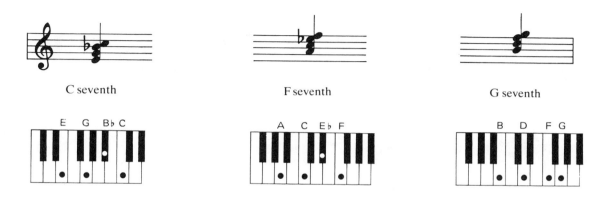

C seventh   F seventh   G seventh

Experiment with the rhythm and tempo

Now try playing 12 bar blues on sixths or sevenths in the rhythm that you feel—say,

> *playing slowly:* two chords per bar with the right hand but keeping one note held for four beats in each bar with the left hand.
>
> *or playing fast:* eight chords per bar with the right hand but keeping one note held for four beats in each bar with the left hand.

Try 12 bar blues in different keys:

F, using the chords

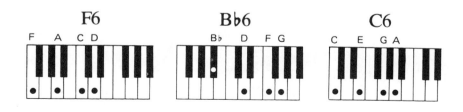

F6   **B♭6**   **C6**

or

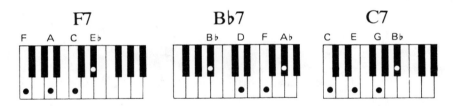

or G, using the chords

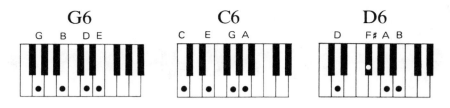

or

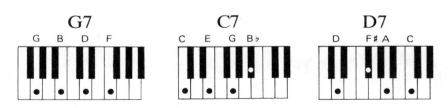

and so on.

Vary the playing between left and right hands: play single notes with the left hand as outlined, or play chords with the left hand (2 or 4 in a bar) and play single notes from the chords with the right hand.

In time you will return to 12 bar blues to play boogie woogie, improvise to, play early songs, or play rock'n roll songs. It sometimes appears as 24 bars which is a version where each bar is played twice to make up the total of 24 bars in all.

SUMMARY

The primary chords in any key are the major chords based on the I, IV, and V notes of the particular scale. These are the most common chords in music. They are the chords used in 12 bar blues which is a set sequence of these three chords played for a total of 12 bars.

Knowing this, 12 bar blues can be played in any key taking the I, IV, and V chords. We can use this structure to increase familiarity with the basic chords and to achieve a certain rhythmic interplay between the hands. Further embellishments from later lessons can then be applied and in time your ability to use 12 bar blues will increase.

Lesson 5

Playing by Chords from Music

INTRODUCTION

The choice of sheet or album music to buy is yours entirely, but it should have chord symbols written below or above the staves. There are some books available that give only the single note melody line and the chord symbols, and these are ideal.

Playing from music, using the chord approach gives greater flexibility than playing the "set" arrangement. Particularly with pop music, the sheet music is sometimes a poor reflection of the sound created on recordings. Chords enable you to put your own interpretation to the music, or to experiment, in order to match the sound and rhythm that you have heard, or wish to achieve.

Having played a piece using chords, transposing can be easier—refer to the Transposing chart in Appendix III.

Other examples of the freedom that playing by chords gives are that it becomes easier to "back" other instruments, or voice, and that once the chord pattern is established in your mind, improvisation possibilities present themselves more naturally.

In reading from sheet or album music, it will soon be realized that there are different ways of denoting a chord, and different symbols for the same chord will be met. Reference should be made to the Chord symbol chart in Appendix II if there is any doubt about what a particular chord symbol means.

Help with other difficulties encountered in written music (for example reading key signatures) will be found in the Basic review course in Appendix I, or in earlier lessons.

Besides symbols for chords, or words and phrases indicating tempo and mood, others will be encountered which specify which sections of music are to be repeated or omitted. The most common ones are as follows:

Phrase/symbol	Meaning
Da Capo D.C.	Repeat from the beginning
D.C. al Segno	Repeat from the beginning to the sign 𝄋
Dal Segno D.S.	From the sign 𝄋
D.S. al Coda	Repeat from the sign 𝄋 until you come to the phrase "To Coda ⊕"
To Coda ⊕	Next play the music marked "⊕ Coda"
⊕ Coda	Indicates the start of the Coda section
ːǁ	Repeat from the sign ǁː, or if there is no such sign, repeat from the beginning
⌐1⌐ ⌐2⌐	First time through, play the music covered by ⌐1⌐ then repeat as specified and omit the music covered by ⌐1⌐ and play that covered by ⌐2⌐

THE METHOD

I suggest that the music and chord symbols be tackled in the following way:

1. First play the melody line with the right hand until you are familiar with the tune.

2. Then, separately, play the chord with the left hand. Where necessary, go back to basics to work out the chord.

To start with, do not feel that you have to play every chord in a bar or add all the notes given. You will be able to do that eventually, but aim now for simple harmonies, say, by playing only the first and third chords if four different chords are given in a bar. Once you become familiar with the piece and the chord changes, the further chords/notes can be added.

3. Then play the left and right hand together in a simple rhythm.

4. When you have the feel of the piece of music, vary the mixture so that it might be:

a. single notes in the left hand;

b. *or* inverted chords in the left hand;

c. *or* notes from the chords added to the right hand below the melody note;

d. *or* left and right hands playing chords with you singing the song.

5. Work on it until the rhythm, tempo, and sound satisfy you.

Progress may be a little slow at first, but as dexterity and familiarity with chords increase, it will become easier. Even to start with, it is far easier than reading all the "dots," and, without too much difficulty, you will be playing the pieces all the way through. Because they will be tunes/songs that you like, you will be able to practice them with some sort of end product in mind, and each time through will be easier than the last.

PRACTICAL ILLUSTRATIONS

I have chosen a few bars from several songs to illustrate the basic approach that should be adopted in playing from music using chords. You can try each example, or merely pick out the ones that appeal to you. I have given the chord positions, but you should be able to work these out for yourself and you should attempt to do so even with these exercises. The approach should be as outlined above:

1. play the melody with the right hand;
2. play the chords with the left hand;
3. play left and right hand together—playing the chords with the left hand only once in each bar;
4. play left and right hands together—playing the chords with the left hand as many times in each bar as seems appropriate;
5. when you have played any of these songs in the straightforward way of melody with the right hand and chords with the left hand, vary this so that you play only the root of the chord with the left hand and add notes from the chords to the melody line played with the right hand. The notes added should be below the melody note and as close as possible to it. For example, for "Hey Jude":

The combinations are endless and in the last analysis purely a question of personal preference. Ask yourself the questions: What does it sound like? Does it feel "right"? Is the sound full enough, or could more notes be added in the left or right hands? etc., and make adjustments accordingly. Inevitably, you will make comparisons with versions of the song you have heard elsewhere. It may not be possible to capture, say, the sound created on record using electronic equipment, but the chord approach gives sufficient flexibility to arrive at a version which you will be content to play.

In all songs, it helps if you sing along with the piano and that in turn means that it is not so necessary to play the melody on the piano, and your hands are liberated to further experiment with sounds.

Oh! Susanna

Melody notes with the right hand

Chords with the left hand (at first try 1 in a bar, then later 2 in a bar)

I__ come from Al - a - bam - a wid me ban - jo on my knee. I'm_
F   F   F   C7

gwine to Lou - si - an - a my true love for to see. It____
F   F   F   C7   F

rained all day the night I left the weath - er it was dry. The__
F   F   F   C7

sun so hot I froze to death, Su - san - na don't you cry.
F   F   F   C7   F

Hey Jude

Words and Music by John Lennon & Paul McCartney

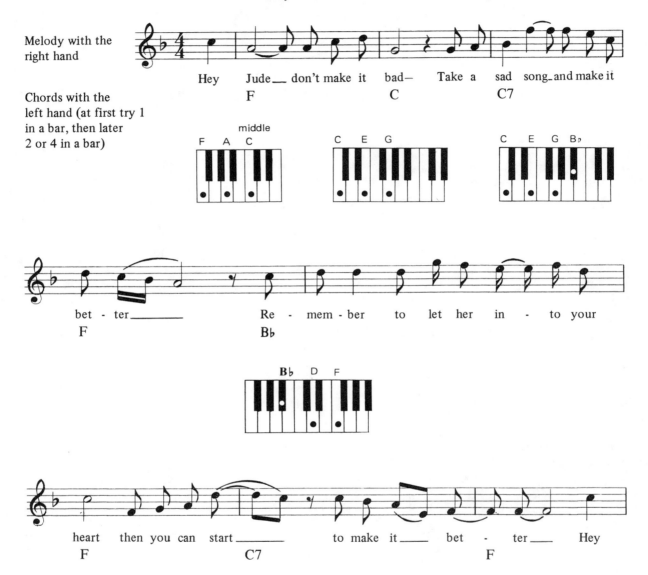

Melody with the right hand

Hey Jude— don't make it bad— Take a sad song and make it

F   C   C7

Chords with the left hand (at first try 1 in a bar, then later 2 or 4 in a bar)

bet - ter_____ Re - mem - ber to let her in - to your

F   Bb

heart then you can start_____ to make it___ bet - ter___ Hey

F   C7   F

Grease

Words and Music by Barry Gibb

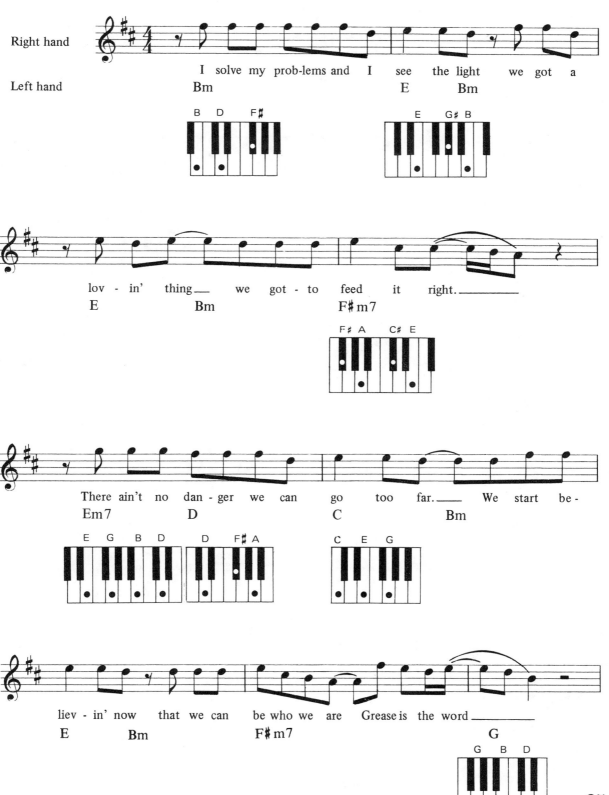

How Deep Is Your Love

Words and Music by Barry, Robin, & Maurice Gibb

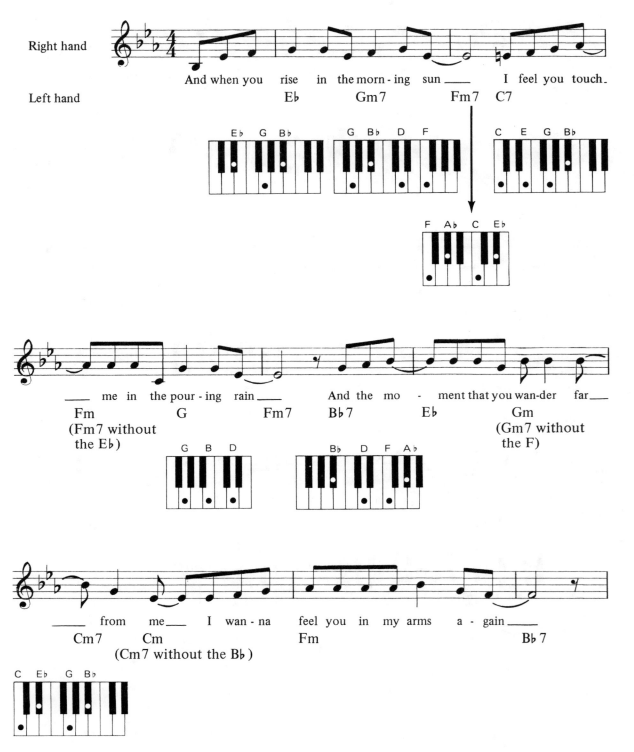

Body and Soul

Words by Robert Sour, Edward Heyman, & Frank Eyton; Music by John W. Green

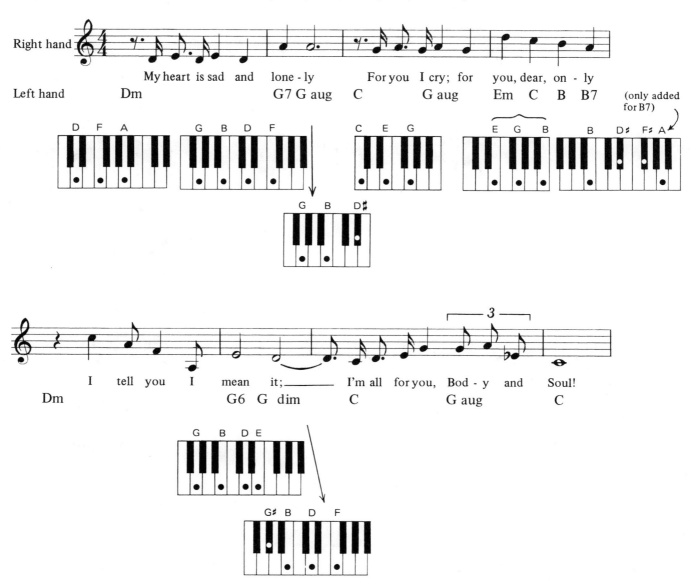

Let's Call the Whole Thing Off

Words by Ira Gershwin; Music by George Gershwin

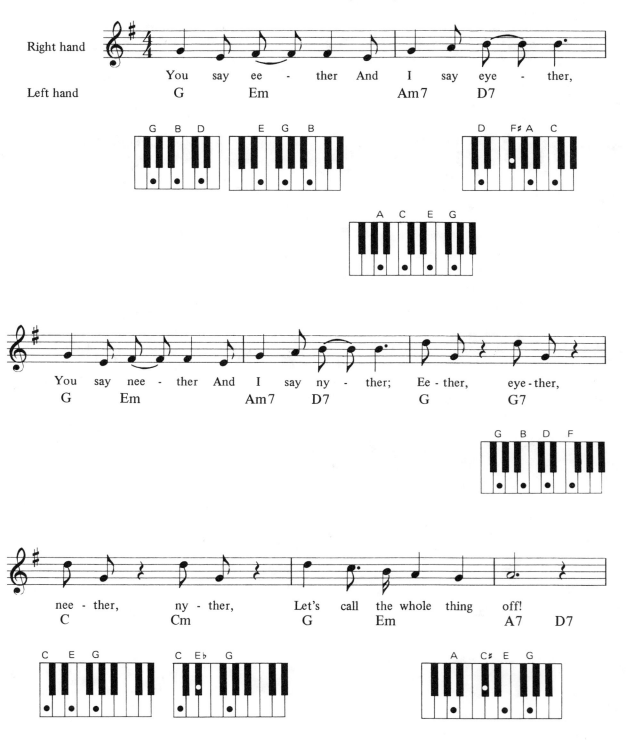

Right hand

Left hand

You say ee - ther And I say eye - ther,

G   Em   Am7   D7

You say nee - ther And I say ny - ther; Ee - ther, eye - ther,

G   Em   Am7   D7   G   G7

nee - ther, ny - ther, Let's call the whole thing off!

C   Cm   G   Em   A7   D7

SUMMARY

With a knowledge of basic and further chords, music that has chord symbols can be played using chords. With a little practice you will be able to play, with both hands, the tunes and songs that you like, in your own style.

Buy music that has chord symbols, then use the approach contained in this lesson: play the melody with the right hand and the chords with the left hand; then experiment with the mixture adding to, or subtracting from, the notes played with either hand until it sounds right to you.

In time you will be able to play the chords automatically and the melody with left and/or right hands as appropriate.

Lesson 6

Playing Chords by Ear; Jazz

INTRODUCTION

Playing by ear is really the ability to pick out a tune and surround it by chords.

Jazz, in its less way-out forms, is improvising to a given chord sequence in the mood that the known tune has created or the pianist wishes to express.

In both, the most commonly used chords have a certain relationship with each other, whatever the key, and these will be briefly discussed here.

A REVIEW
OF COMMON CHORDS

Major chords

It has been seen that in any key the most used chords are the fundamental chords of the I, IV, and V notes of the scale.

In the key of C, these are C, F, and G;
In the key of F, these are F, B♭, and C;
In the key of E♭, they are E♭, A♭, and B♭,

with added notes or amendments as appropriate.

Relative minors

These are the minor chords that complement in sound particular major chords.

The relative minor chord of a major chord is to be found a minor third (4 half steps inclusive) down from the root note of the major chord.

Thus the relative minor of C major is A minor:

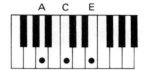
a minor third

That it is a minor third can be seen in that the chord of A minor has the notes:

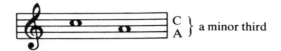

In other words, take A major, lower the third for A minor. The interval between A and C natural (the lowered third) is a minor third. The root note of a major chord is the lowered third note of its relative minor chord.

From other majors the relative minors would be:

Play these chords and hear their relationship.

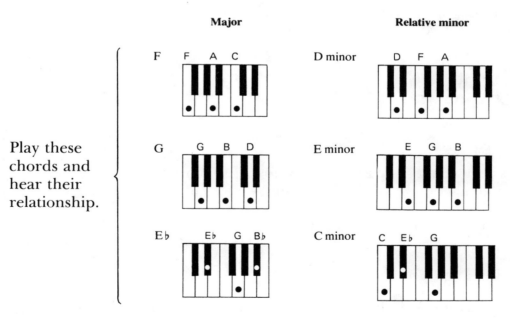

Relative minors have the same key signatures as their majors do.

II minor chords

In any key, it is also common to find that music written in that key uses, besides relative minor chords, the minor chord formed on the second note of the major scale of that key.

Thus in C, D minor (the minor chord formed on the second note, D, of the major scale of C) would be likely to appear as well as the fundamental chords C, F, and G (the I, IV, and V) and the relative minor A minor.

Similarly in F, besides F, B♭, and C (the I, IV, and V chords) and the relative minor, D minor, G minor might appear—G minor being the chord formed on the second note of the scale of F major.

And so on.

The Transposing chart will help you to work out the relative and II minors, in any key, that correspond to those shown above.

CHORD PROGRESSIONS

You will have played the progression, for example, between C, F, and G major chords as in 12 bar blues, but now play the following chords and note their relationship in sound:

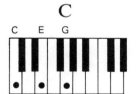

C

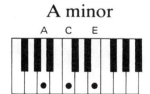

A minor

F

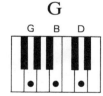

G

then

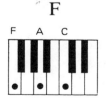

F

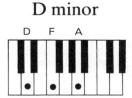

D minor

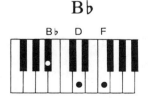

B♭

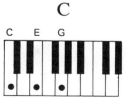

C

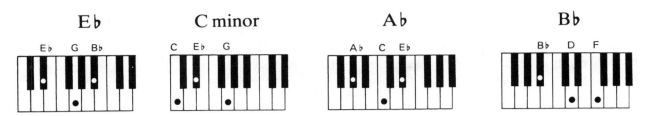

and so on in different keys.

Now play the following chords—as above, but with the different chords marked:

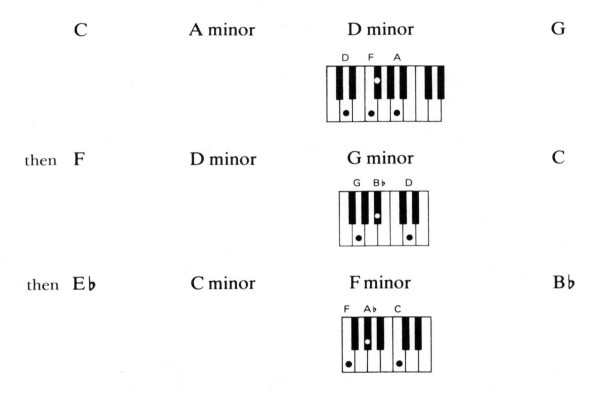

and so on in different keys.

Playing each block of four or five chords as above demonstrates that the chords sound "right" with each other and you will readily appreciate that they could appear together in the same piece of music.

Many songs revolve round these four or five chords, which can of course be played in any sequence; "Blowin' In The Wind," "Blue Moon," etc. The list is endless and you will be able to add to it with ease. The examples given in Lesson 5 demonstrate this. Another common chord progression, especially in current songs, is from a minor to a major, as in:

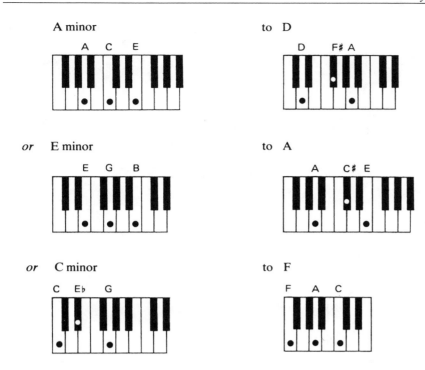

The progression is from the minor chord to the major chord a fourth up from the root note of the minor chord.

It is also important to remember that this progression can be used even with other notes being added to the minor and major chords involved. The examples below illustrate this point and also how chords can be used in their inverted positions to give a smoother transition, not only in fingering, but also in sound.

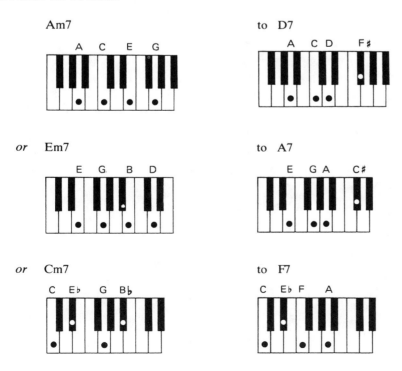

This progression is very commonly used in many popular songs, in the songs used in lesson 5 and, for example, in this extract from "Autumn Leaves":

The fall-ing leaves — Drift by my win-dow ——
Am7   D7   G

PLAYING BY EAR

This should be your approach to songs or tunes that you attempt to play by ear:

1. First play the melody line with the right hand and try to identify the key, for example, by singing the final note of the piece (or otherwise determining the "resting place" of the piece) and then playing that note on the piano, as this will give you the keynote. If you are not so familiar with the chords in the key that you have hit on, raise or lower the melody line until it is in a key you are happy with.

2. Then, put chords to the melody line by trying chords with the left hand. Think first of the fundamental chords: the I, IV, and V, and the basic chords on those notes; and then try the relative and II minors. Work on the principle that the melody note is one of the notes that makes up the chord. A few chords will seem to fit, but select the one that sounds the best. You may have to try many chords—majors, minors, diminished, augmented, major sevenths, sevenths, etc., until you find the right one. The tune itself will dictate when to change chords.

NOTE Don't be thrown off course if you have difficulty with finding the key and the chords—this will take a few attempts at first but should get easier. You may find a key that you are happiest in both with regard to the tune (or perhaps a comfortable singing range) and the chords. Noel Coward, I believe, was happiest in the key of A flat!

3. Now add notes from the chosen chords to the right hand and experiment with right and left hand notes and rhythm until you get the piece to sound "right."

As your dexterity increases and you get more practice in putting chords to tunes, it will become easier to pick up and play tunes by ear. In this way, it will be possible to learn songs, etc., from radio or records. One difficulty that might be encountered here is that unless your piano is at concert pitch, playing along with the record might present some problems.

With these various chords and their relationships in mind, we can now try to work out a simple tune and put chords to it using the approach outlined above. The example used here is chosen because it is probably a tune that most people know, but the approach is the same for any piece of music that you wish to play by ear.

With the right hand try to play the tune of "She'll Be Comin' 'Round the Mountain." Try to do this *at this point,* without looking at the music written out for it, but so that we remain in the same key—you can check later on how you are doing from the music. Start the tune on the note G above middle C as the first note of the tune.

Man: Do you know you're ugly?
Pianist: No, but you whistle it and I'll try to pick it up.

While playing it, you will have realized that in the melody you play, there are no sharps or flats and the final note, and natural "resting place" of the piece is the note of C—this means in this instance that we are in the key of C.

Immediately, you should think of the fundamental or "primary" major chords made of notes from the scale of C major: in other words, I, IV, and V chords of C, F, and G. The other chords of A minor (the relative minor) and D minor (the minor based on the second note of the scale) should also come to mind. If the tune had been picked out in another key, the corresponding chords in that key should spring to mind.

Now with the left hand, try putting the fundamental chords to the tune—with the principle that the melody note being played is one of the three notes (the first, third, or fifth) of a chord.

So the first main note here is C—a note appearing in the chords of C, F, and A minor; try them all—but fairly obviously the one that fits is C itself. Move in this way through the piece, choosing the relevant chords by reference to their notes and the melody note, and selecting the one that gives the required sound. Do not attempt to put chords under too many notes because the chord changes in this piece are not frequent. Test your result with the written version of the tune and chords as shown opposite.

Try to play this as rhythmically as possible. At first, with the right hand playing only the melody line and the left hand the chords. Now add notes from the chords to the right hand, below the melody line, and play single notes or chords with the left hand. Vary the mixture until you are satisfied with the sound.

She'll Be Comin' 'Round the Mountain

Right hand

She'll be com - in' 'round the moun-tain when she comes ___ she'll be

Left hand   C   /   C   /   C   C

com - in' 'round the moun - tain when she comes ___ she'll be com - in' 'round the
C   /   C   /   G7   G7   C   /

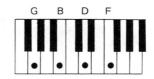

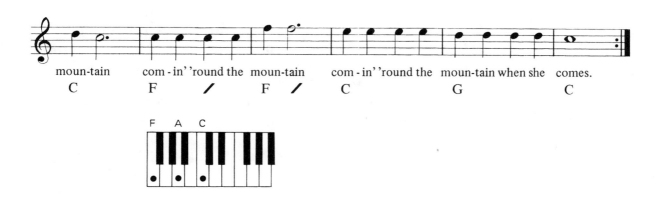

moun-tain   com - in' 'round the moun-tain   com - in' 'round the moun-tain when she comes.
C   F   /   F   /   C   G   C

81

JAZZ OR IMPROVISING

Familiarity with chords and their uses outlined in this and preceding lessons will form a springboard into jazz and improvising. This section briefly outlines the basic approach to adopt.

What is important to bear in mind is the sequence of chords of the tune/song. Your approach to improvising around or jazzing up a melody should be to play the piece—tune and chords—fairly straight at first, as written or as worked out by ear, to become familiar with the sequence of chords: the order in which they are played and when the changes occur. The examples in Lesson 5 can be used as bases for improvisation of the few bars of melody given.

Then, playing the same sequence of chords, say in the left hand, you should try with the right hand to take odd notes from the melody line and run into other notes from the chords being played. Bear in mind, for sharps and flats and the notes affected, the key that the piece is in. However, do not be too strict, for after all this is improvisation. With the right hand, play notes above or below the melody line and use the range of the keyboard fully. Playing chords, inverted as needs be, can often be effective for the right hand.

At all times the sequence of chords should be kept in mind and the notes that make up those chords should be kept foremost. You should try to use chords to "back" your own singing of the song or another instrument, and then, after the first time through, jazz the tune up by taking notes from the melody line and running into notes from the chords, or adding notes in between notes of the melody.

In time, dexterity will increase and so will your ability to improvise around a given chord sequence. You may be able then to devise your own chord sequences and improvisations.

Try to use 12 bar blues as much as possible: the chord sequence is fairly easy to remember and free improvisation can be practiced. For example, try this extract from "Dippermouth Blues" as a basis for improvisation, by playing it at first as it is written and then using the chords so as to support a free-ranging right hand.

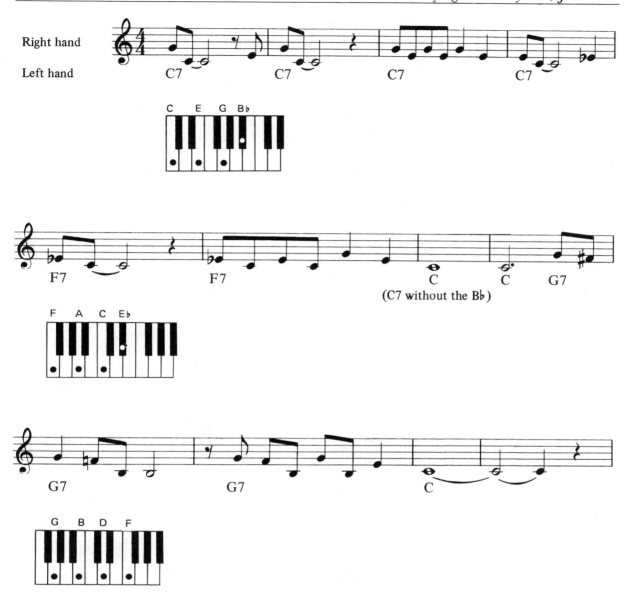

It can be seen and heard in the melody of "Dippermouth Blues" that it contains lowered thirds and sevenths. These are the "blue" notes that give blues melodies and improvisations their distinctive sound. (*Bebop* musicians also introduced the lowered fifth and this then became a "blue" note).

The blues have been a constant source of inspiration and the 12 bar blues structure has been used throughout the history of jazz, because it is so fundamental and flexible a form. However, any chord progression, be it from a popular song or that of an own composition can be used as a basis for improvisation.

Jazz is constantly evolving and the variety of styles in rhythm, melody, harmony, and use of chords is infinite. In early piano jazz, the chords used tended to be in their more basic form, but over the years, the use of chords has become more sophisticated by varying the notes being added to give different harmonies and chord progressions.

In improvising, it is important to experiment with rhythm and harmony to develop your own style, or styles, of playing and in this respect, the following "profiles" (which concentrate on piano aspects) of different styles indicate the variety.

Ragtime

Ragtime (literally "ragged" time) became popular towards the end of the nineteenth century and was essentially composed piano music, inspired partly by military marches and the cakewalk, but, as with all jazz, having many musical influences. The rhythm of ragtime is strict 2 or 4 time, with the left hand playing single notes, octaves, or tenths on the 1st and 3rd beats in the bar, and the notes of the I, IV, and V chords on the 2nd and 4th beats. The right hand is used for the melody, for improvisation and to create cross rhythms and syncopation. Piano exponents of ragtime include Scott Joplin and Jelly Roll Morton, who, along with pianists like James P. Johnson, Willie "The Lion" Smith, and the young Fats Waller, kept the ragtime tradition alive during the 1920s.

New Orleans and Chicago Styles

In *New Orleans* and *Chicago* styles, jazz developed into the 1920s its traditional ("trad") image. Many different musical influences had met and mixed in New Orleans and found a jazz expression, but when New Orleans became a war port during the First World War, the red light district of Storyville was closed and many musicians moved up to Chicago, where several important recordings of New Orleans jazz were made, and where the style was modified into what is known as the Chicago style. In both, the melodic excitement is created by cornet, or trumpet, clarinet and trombone, with the piano used more as a rhythm instrument. In New Orleans, the rhythm emphasizes the 1st and 3rd beats, but in Chicago, although still strong, the accent moved from the 1st and 3rd, to the 2nd and 4th beats. This

Chicago development leads into the rhythm of *Swing*. The most common chord pattern was still 12 bar blues, but Chicago style is not such a melodic melange as New Orleans and introduced more of the soloist approach to jazz. Piano exponents of New Orleans include Jelly Roll Morton and of Chicago, Earl Hines.

Boogie Woogie

Boogie woogie, again a blues based jazz form almost exclusively in 12 bar structure, was popularized in Chicago. The left hand is used to play a repeated pattern on the piano using I, IV, and V chords while the right hand improvises and adds to the rhythmic effect. Exponents include Meade Lux Lewis, Memphis Slim, Jimmy Yancey, and Pinetop Smith (whose "Pinetop's Boogie Woogie" gave the style its name).

Swing

The *Swing* era of the 1930s saw the growth of big bands. Although 12 bar blues was still used as a basis, popular songs (often in 32 bar form) became jazz standards. The chords were more sophisticated, with major sevenths, ninths, elevenths, etc. being used, as well as there being an increased use of chromatic chords (i.e., chords containing notes which are not part of the scale of the key of the piece of music). The rhythm of swing was more "floating" than previously had been used, and it is also known as 4 beat jazz, hence the use of the term "swing." Solos continued to be important and, for the piano, might be said to be characterised by the "stride" piano style, in which the left hand strides, as in Ragtime, from single notes, octaves, or tenths, to chords, but with the right hand used to improvise much more freely than in *ragtime*. Piano exponents include Fats Waller and Teddy Wilson.

Bebop

With *Bebop* (deriving its name either from the attempt to sing the notes of the flattened fifth interval, or from the use of two short notes to round off a solo), more experimentation, in reaction to the orthodoxy of *swing,* resulted in much freer harmonies, melodies, and rhythms being created, often to self-composed themes. The flattened fifth became a feature, but, more than this, the use of passing notes and a more chromatic interpretation of chords gave greater freedom and fluidity in the use of chords. The piano was used for more single note melody playing with the right hand and subtler underpinning chords played with the left hand. The stride piano style was dropped and the bass line left to the string bass. Piano exponents include Theolonius Monk, Clyde Hart, and Bud Powell.

Experimental Jazz

In *Cool Jazz* in the 1950s, Dave Brubeck, for example, with more experimentation with time signatures and more relaxed rhythms, built on *Bebop* styles. This more relaxed approach led to the development of *Free Jazz* in the 1960s and beyond, with no restrictions as to rhythm, tonality, melody, and harmony. *Electric Jazz* has seen the widespread use of electric pianos, organs, and electric keyboards as well as fusions with rock and soul. "Piano" exponents of Free or Electric Jazz, or both, include Chick Corea, Herbie Hancock, Keith Jarrett, and Cecil Taylor.

SUMMARY

I have reviewed the most common chords: the three chord trick (I, IV, and V chords), the relative and related minors, and outlined their relationship.

Certain chord progressions in addition to 12 bar blues have been illustrated.

The way of putting chords to a tune has been outlined and improvising has been shown to be basically a process of keeping to a chord sequence but extemporizing around those chords in and around the known melody.

This book has sought only to introduce the potential of chords and give a system for playing them and hints on applying them. Your own enthusiasm, style, the example of others (from records or concerts) and practice by yourself or with others, will help you to develop as a pianist who plays the piano by chords, especially in the area of improvisation.

My object has been to:

1. give a system for working out and playing chords;
2. suggest an easy way of playing from music using chord symbols;
3. give an introduction to playing by ear and improvising, showing how chords are the basis for both;
4. make the piano more approachable and comprehensible as a means of musical expression;
5. show the importance of thinking in chords and playing by chords.

Appendices

APPENDIX I:
BASIC REVIEW COURSE

The ground covered is:

1. the names of the notes and their positions on the piano, treble and bass clefs
2. note and rest values and time signatures
3. certain musical terms
4. scales and key signatures

**Names of notes
and their positions on the piano,
treble and bass clefs**

1. The keyboard (Most pianos have 7 octaves, A to A.)

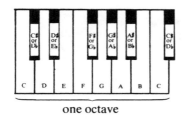

one octave

2. The notes from middle C upwards are usually written in the *treble clef* and the notes below middle C usually in the *bass clef*

3. The notes are written thus:

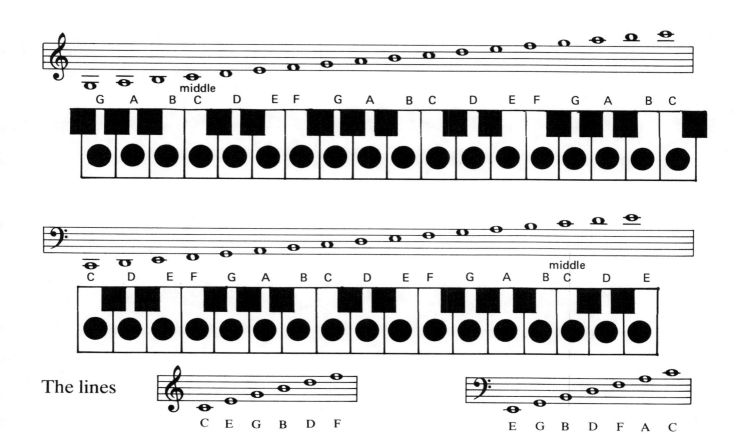

The lines

C E G B D F

E G B D F A C

The spaces

D F A C E G

F A C E G B

It can be seen that the notes in the bass clef are written one space or line down from the equivalent note in the treble clef.

Note and rest values and time signatures

Note	Shape	Rest
whole note	𝅝	▬
half note	𝅗𝅥	▬
quarter note	♩	𝄽 or 𝄾
eighth note	♪	𝄾
sixteenth note	𝅘𝅥𝅯	𝄾
thirty-second note	𝅘𝅥𝅰	𝄾

Think of it as the quarter note being the basic measure = 1 beat

then the half note (= 2 quarter notes)   = 2 beats

the whole note (× 4 quarter notes or 2 half notes)   = 4 beats

the eighth note (× ½ quarter note)   = ½ beat

the sixteenth note (× ¼ quarter note)   = ¼ beat

the thirty-second note (× ⅛ quarter note)   = ⅛ beat

Dotted notes/rests

A dot placed after a note or a rest increases its value by one half. Thus a dotted quarter note ♩.= 1½ quarter notes; and a dotted rest 𝄽•= rest for the duration of 1½ quarter notes.

Tie

A tie between 2 notes, as in ♩⌣♪, means the note is held for 1½ beats, but not played twice. This only applies to the same notes written.

Do not confuse this with *a phrase*, as in ♫♩𝅝, which is a grouping of notes.

Triplets

♫♪ This means that the three notes are to be played in the time that 2 would be played, i.e. here, for 1 quarter note value (× 2 eighth notes), not 1½ quarter notes (× 3 eighth notes).

Bars and time signatures

Music is written in bars and the number of beats in each bar is denoted at the beginning of a piece by a *time signature*. For example:

$\frac{2}{4}$ means two quarter note beats to a bar.

$\frac{4}{4}$ means four quarter note beats to a bar = Common Time (C).

$\frac{2}{2}$ means two half note beats to a bar.

$\frac{6}{8}$ means six eighth note beats to a bar.

For time signatures, the top figure denotes the number of beats and the bottom figure the measure of each beat. The whole note is the basic measure for the latter: thus 4 quarter notes = 1 whole note and the quarter note measure is 4.

Certain musical terms

A *half step* is the smallest distance between two notes: e.g. between C and C♯; C♯ and D; E and F; B and C.

A *whole step* consists of two half steps.

The *sharp* ♯ raises a note one half step.

The *flat* ♭ lowers a note one half step.

The *natural* ♮ restores the note to its original pitch.

A *scale* is a succession of notes starting from a *tonic* (the keynote of the scale) e.g. the tonic of the scale of C major is the note C.

Scales and key signatures

Scales

From any tonic, major or minor scales have the same intervals between their notes as the corresponding scales that start on other tonics.

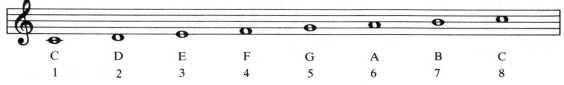

C major

whole step whole step half step whole step whole step whole step half step

C   D   E   F   G   A   B   C
1   2   3   4   5   6   7   8

Between the third and fourth notes of the scale and the seventh and eighth notes, the gap (interval) is a half step, and between other notes a whole step.

This applies to any scale. In order to preserve this spacing, it is necessary in all other scales to raise or lower certain notes.

Thus in the scale of G (running from the key note G), to obtain an interval of a half step between the seventh and eighth notes, the F must be raised.

G major

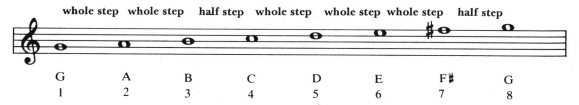

For all scales, intervals are the same as above: whole step, whole step, half step, whole step, whole step, whole step, half step.

The sharps and flats necessary to maintain these intervals are grouped together at the beginning of each stave of music, immediately after the clef. This grouping is called a *key signature* and means that the notes specified are to be lowered or raised throughout unless naturalized.

Table showing key signatures for majors and minors

NOTE I have shown all key signatures but the last three sharp and flat signatures will not be met very often.

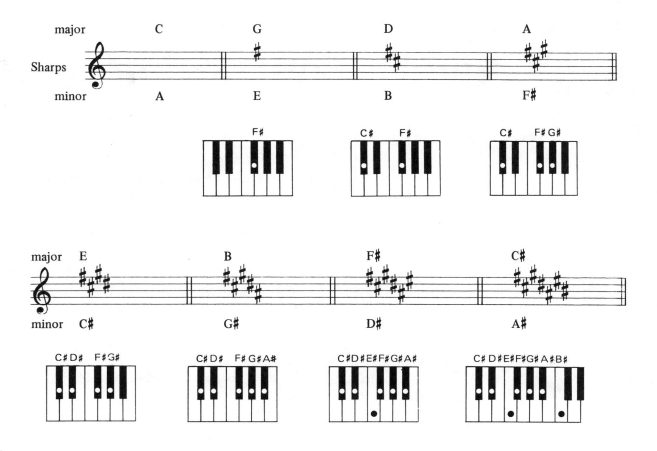

To read the key from a sharp key signature: take the last sharp of the key signature and move one half step up to get the name of the key. E.g., take the key signature with three sharps: the last is G♯—move up a half step to note A, and A is the name of the key.

The minors shown are the relative minors to the majors and have the same key signature. So if the piece is in a minor mood, the key will be minor.

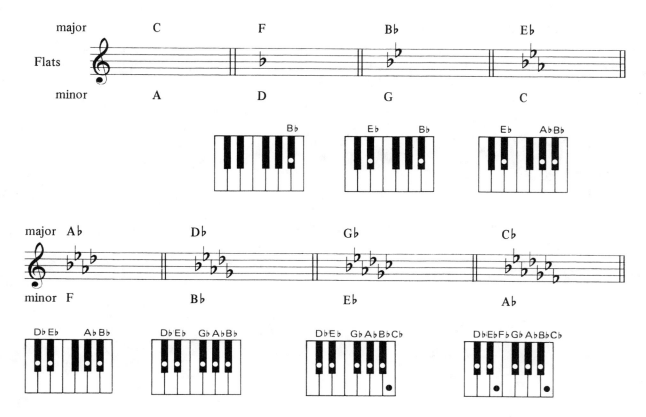

To read the key from a flat signature: take the next to last flat of the key signature and that is the name of the key. E.g., take the key signature that has four flats. The next to the last is A♭ and that is the name of the key. The minors shown are the relative minors and have the same key signature as their majors.

Summary

The aim of this Appendix has been to provide a review of certain points that should make reading a one note melody line easier and to give the basic knowledge required to make the best use of this book.

APPENDIX II:
CHORD SYMBOL CHART

This is a guide to shorthand chord symbols.

NOTE I have used C as the example throughout, but the symbols apply to any key: e.g., F or E♭ could be substituted throughout.

Symbol	Chord	Symbol	Chord
C	basic chord C major	Cm9 *or* C min 9	C minor with added ninth
Cm *or* Cmin	basic chord C minor	C7+5 *or* C7♯5 *or* C7 aug 5	C major with lowered seventh and raised fifth
C+ *or* C+5 *or* Caug *or* Caug5	basic chord C augmented	C min 7+5 *or* Cm7♯5 *or* Cm7 aug5	C minor with lowered seventh and raised fifth
C− *or* C° *or* Cdim *or* Cdim7	basic chord C diminished	C7−5 *or* C7♭5 *or* C7dim5	C major with lowered seventh and lowered fifth
C6 *or* Cadd6	C major with added sixth	Cm7−5 *or* Cm7♭5 *or* Cm7dim5	C minor with lowered seventh and lowered fifth
C9 *or* C add 9	C major with added ninth	C sus 4 *or* C sus F	C major with the fourth note (F) added
C maj 7	C major with added major seventh	C−9 *or* C♭9	C major with a lowered ninth
C7	C major with added seventh	C+9 *or* Caug9	C augmented with an added ninth
Cm6 *or* C−6 *or* Cmin6	C minor with added sixth	C♯ 9	C major with a raised ninth
		C13	C major with added thirteenth
Cm7 *or* C−7 *or* Cmin7	C minor with added lowered seventh	C13♭9	C major with thirteenth and lowered ninth
C$^9_7$	C major with added lowered seventh and ninth	C$^9_6$	C major with added sixth and ninth
C7−9 *or* C7♭9	C major with added lowered seventh and lowered ninth	And other variations to the various symbols	There is a great deal of variety in the symbols that can be used to denote the required chord, as is indicated in this table which covers only the most common symbols used. Any others, you should be able to work out.
C with brackets say, (6) *or* (7) *or* (+5) *or* (min) *or* (B♭ bass)	C major or other chord with the note that is specified in the brackets added		
C (G bass) *or* C(G)	Play the chord of C but with the note specified in brackets as the base		

APPENDIX III:
TRANSPOSING CHART

To be used in transposing notes or chords from one key to another.

Method: take the existing key, then move horizontally to the required key. The required note or chord in the new key is on the same line as the note in the old key. You can move horizontally forwards or backwards into new keys.

Vertically, I have written the notes of the scales in the different keys.

NOTE I have only gone to the key of B major in sharps and D♭ in flats as being the limit of the chart's usefulness.

	Sharps						Flats				
Key of	**C**	**G**	**D**	**A**	**E**	**B**	**F**	**B♭**	**E♭**	**A♭**	**D♭**
	D	A	E	B	F♯	C♯	G	C	F	B♭	E♭
	E	B	F♯	C♯	G♯	D♯	A	D	G	C	F
	F	C	G	D	A	E	B♭	E♭	A♭	D♭	G♭
	G	D	A	E	B	F♯	C	F	B♭	E♭	A♭
	A	E	B	F♯	C♯	G♯	D	G	C	F	B♭
	B	F♯	C♯	G♯	D♯	A♯	E	A	D	G	C
	C	G	D	A	E	B	F	B♭	E♭	A♭	D♭

Examples: If we were in the key of C and wished to play in A, the corresponding chord to A minor in the key of C, is F minor (moving horizontally) in the key of A. If we were in E♭ and wished to be in B: the note A♭ in the key of E♭ would be E in the key of B and the chord A♭ minor would be E minor.

APPENDIX IV:
CHORD EXAMPLES

It is important to be able to work out chords rather than trying to memorize chord positions.

However, as an aid to learning during the initial stages of understanding chords and how to use them, the following chord chart sets out, for easy reference, some of the different types of chords in different keys.

Major chords

C major

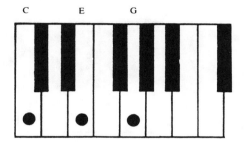

F major

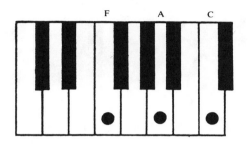

G major

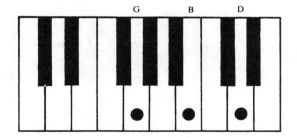

Eb major

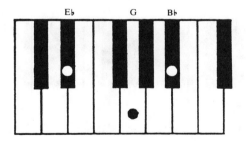

Minor chords

C minor

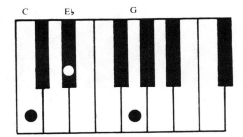

F minor

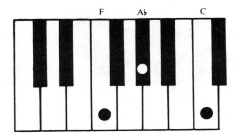

G minor

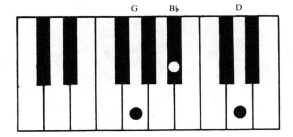

E♭ minor

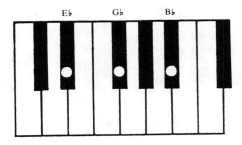

Diminished chords

NOTE The sixth is often added in playing diminished chords, see Sixth chords.

C diminished

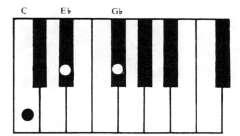

D diminished

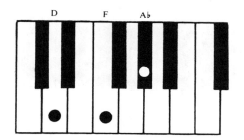

A diminished

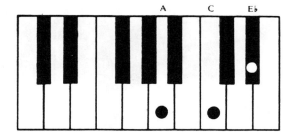

B♭ diminished

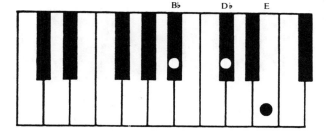

Augmented chords

C augmented

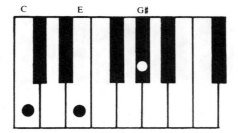

F augmented

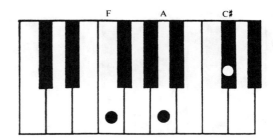

G augmented

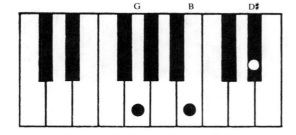

E♭ augmented

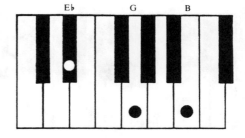

Sixth chords

C sixth

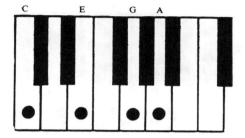

F sixth

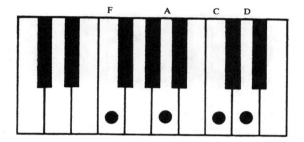

C minor sixth

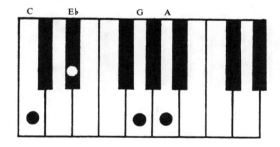

C diminished sixth

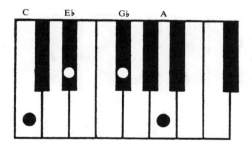

Major seventh chords

C major seventh

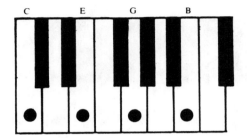

F major seventh

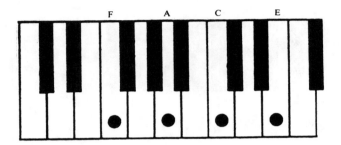

E♭ major seventh

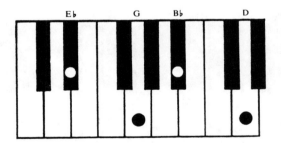

A major seventh

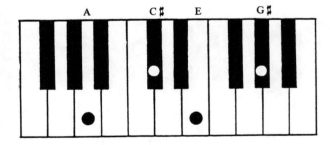

Seventh chords:
major chords with added sevenths

C seventh

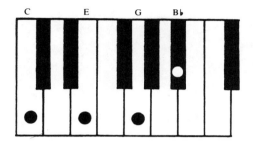

F seventh

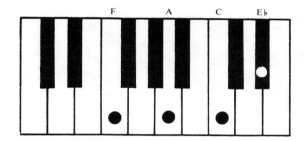

G seventh

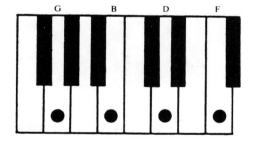

A seventh

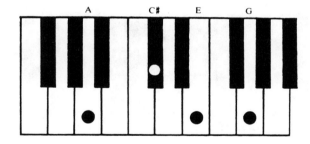

Seventh chords:
minor chords with added sevenths

C minor seventh

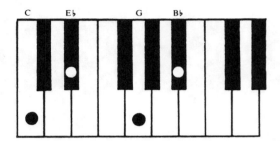

F minor seventh

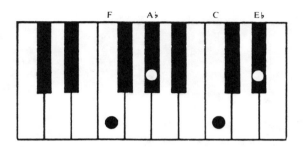

G minor seventh

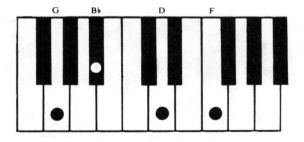

A minor seventh

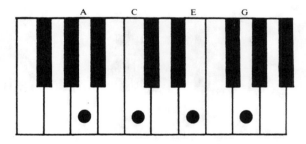

Ninth chords

NOTE The seventh can also be played in ninth chords.

C ninth

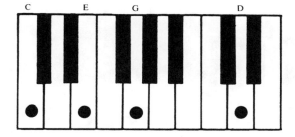

C minor ninth

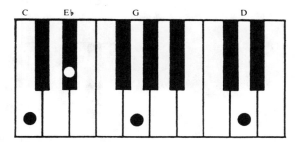

C diminished, ninth

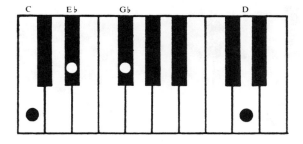

C augmented, ninth

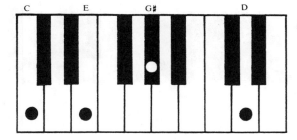

Miscellaneous chords

Virtually any notes can be added to the basic chords and this can be denoted by an appropriate chord symbol (see Appendix II). Such symbols are self-descriptive as indicated in the following examples:

C seventh with an added fourth

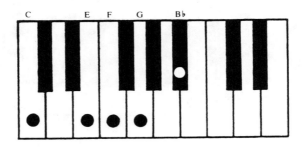

F major with a flattened fifth

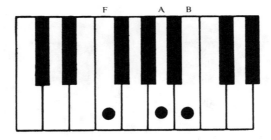

Index